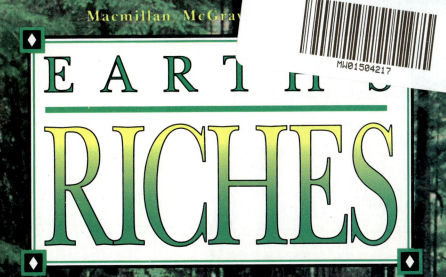

Macmillan/McGraw

EARTH'S
RICHES

AUTHORS

Mary Atwater
The University of Georgia

Prentice Baptiste
University of Houston

Lucy Daniel
Rutherford County Schools

Jay Hackett
University of Northern Colorado

Richard Moyer
University of Michigan, Dearborn

Carol Takemoto
Los Angeles Unified School District

Nancy Wilson
Sacramento Unified School District

Douglas firs in Mt. Hood National Forest, Oregon

Macmillan/McGraw-Hill School Publishing Company
New York   **Columbus**

MACMILLAN / McGRAW-HILL

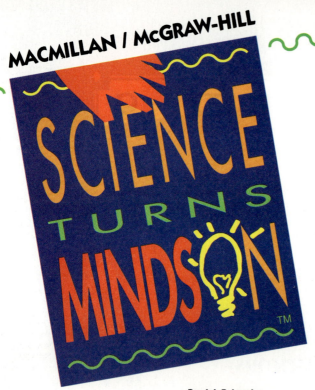

SCIENCE TURNS MINDS ON ™

CONSULTANTS

Assessment:
Mary Hamm
Associate Professor
Department of Elementary Education
San Francisco State University
San Francisco, CA

Cognitive Development:
Pat Guild, Ed.D.
Director, Graduate Programs in Education and
Learning Styles Consultant
Antioch University
Seattle, WA

Kathi Hand, M.A.Ed.
Middle School Teacher and Learning Styles Consultant
Assumption School
Seattle, WA

Derrick R. Lavoie
Assistant Professor of Science Education
Montana State University
Bozeman, MT

Earth Science:
David G. Futch
Associate Professor of Biology
San Diego State University
San Diego, CA

Dr. Shadia Rifai Habbal
Harvard-Smithsonian Center for Astrophysics
Cambridge, MA

Tom Murphree, Ph.D.
Global Systems Studies
Monterey, CA

Suzanne O'Connell
Assistant Professor
Wesleyan University
Middletown, CT

Sidney E. White
Professor of Geology
The Ohio State University
Columbus, OH

Environmental Education:
Cheryl Charles, Ph.D.
Executive Director
Project Wild
Boulder, CO

Gifted:
Dr. James A. Curry
Associate Professor, Graduate Faculty
College of Education, University of Southern Maine
Gorham, ME

Global Education:
M. Eugene Gilliom
Professor of Social Studies and Global Education
The Ohio State University
Columbus, OH

Life Science:
Wyatt W. Anderson
Professor of Genetics
University of Georgia
Athens, GA

Orin G. Gelderloos
Professor of Biology and Professor of Environmental Studies
University of Michigan—Dearborn
Dearborn, MI

Donald C. Lisowy
Education Specialist
New York, NY

Dr. E.K. Merrill
Assistant Professor
University of Wisconsin Center—Rock County
Madison, WI

Literature:
Dr. Donna E. Norton
Texas A&M University
College Station, TX

Macmillan/McGraw-Hill School Division
10 Union Square East
New York, New York 10003
Printed in the United States of America

ISBN 0-02-276129-2/6

6 7 8 9 RRW 99 98 97 96

Mathematics:
Dr. Richard Lodholz
Parkway School District
St. Louis, MO

Middle School Specialist:
Daniel Rodriguez
Principal
Pomona, CA

Misconceptions:
Dr. Charles W. Anderson
Michigan State University
East Lansing, MI

Dr. Edward L. Smith
Michigan State University
East Lansing, MI

Multicultural:
Bernard L. Charles
Senior Vice President
Quality Education for Minorities Network
Washington, DC

Paul B. Janeczko
Poet
Hebron, MA

James R. Murphy
Math Teacher
La Guardia High School
New York, NY

Clifford E. Trafzer
Professor and Chair, Ethnic Studies
University of California, Riverside
Riverside, CA

Physical Science:
Gretchen M. Gillis
Geologist
Maxus Exploration Company
Dallas, TX

Henry C. McBay
Professor of Chemistry
Morehouse College and Clark Atlanta University
Atlanta, GA

Wendell H. Potter
Associate Professor of Physics
Department of Physics
University of California, Davis
Davis, CA

Claudia K. Viehland
Educational Consultant, Chemist
Sigma Chemical Company
St. Louis, MO

Reading:
Charles Temple, Ph.D.
Associate Professor of Education
Hobart and William Smith Colleges
Geneva, NY

Safety:
Janice Sutkus
Program Manager: Education
National Safety Council
Chicago, IL

**Science Technology
and Society (STS):**
William C. Kyle, Jr.
Director, School Mathematics and Science Center
Purdue University
West Lafayette, IN

Social Studies:
Jean Craven
District Coordinator of Curriculum Development
Albuquerque Public Schools
Albuquerque, NM

**Students Acquiring
English:**
Mario Ruiz
Pomona, CA

STUDENT ACTIVITY TESTERS

Alveria Henderson	Andrew Duffy
Kate McGlumphy	Chris Higgins
Katherine Petzinger	Sean Pruitt
John Wirtz	Joanna Huber
Sarah Wittenbrink	John Petzinger

FIELD TEST TEACHERS

Kathy Bowles
Landmark Middle School
Jacksonville, FL

Myra Dietz
#46 School
Rochester, NY

John Gridley
H.L. Harshman Junior High School #101
Indianapolis, IN

Annette Porter
Schenk Middle School
Madison, WI

Connie Boone
Fletcher Middle School
Jacksonville, FL

Theresa Smith
Bates Middle School
Annapolis, MD

Debbie Stamler
Sennett Middle School
Madison, WI

Margaret Tierney
Sennett Middle School
Madison, WI

Mel Pfeiffer
I.P.S. #94
Indianapolis, IN

CONTRIBUTING WRITER

Susan Greiner

ACKNOWLEDGEMENTS

"Adopt A Stream" & "Keep It Cool" from *50 SIMPLE THINGS KIDS CAN DO TO SAVE THE EARTH,* Copyright © 1990 John Cavna. Reprinted with permission of Andrews and McMeel.

HATCHET by Gary Paulsen (New York: Bradbury, 1987).

Ore truck

Earth's Riches

Activities!

Features

 Links

CAREERS

SCIENCE TECHNOLOGY AND Society

Departments

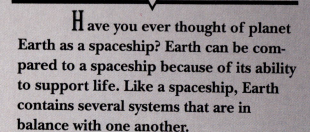

Have you ever thought of planet Earth as a spaceship? Earth can be compared to a spaceship because of its ability to support life. Like a spaceship, Earth contains several systems that are in balance with one another.

In our studies of other planets, we have yet to find another Earth. No other planet that we've seen is covered with so many living things. Many of the inhabitants on Earth have changed, or evolved, over nearly five billion years. Despite the changes, Earth has provided a relatively stable environment for millions of organisms. However, in the past 150 years or so, people have changed the environment and upset this stability. Every living person or thing has an impact on every other living person or thing and on the whole environment.

Soil, forests and their plants, minerals, air, and water are some of Earth's riches.

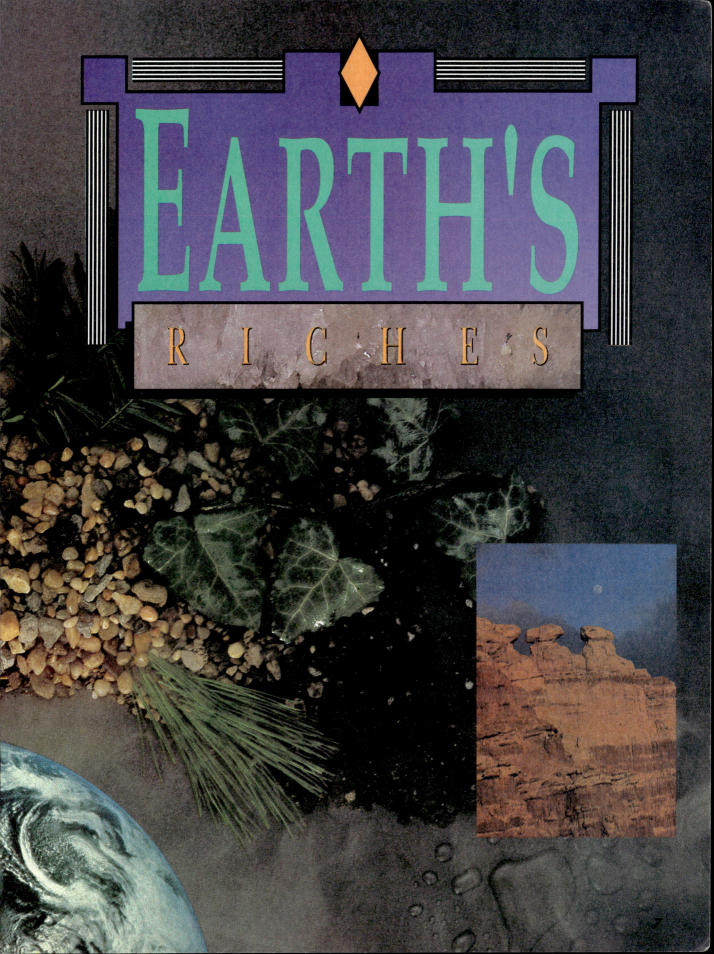

EARTH'S

RICHES

We don't inherit the Earth from our ancestors . . . we borrow it from our children.

Minds On! What does this bumper sticker mean? Imagine a day in the life of your children. What kinds of transportation will they use? What types of food will they eat? Describe a typical day your children may have. Write your descriptions in your *Activity Log* on page 1. Share your ideas with your classmates. ●

Restoring the stability of Earth will take careful observation and planning. People in many countries have begun to join together to preserve Earth's natural resources and to stop polluting Earth's water, air, land and other riches. Every spring since 1970, for example, Earth Day has been celebrated. What does Earth Day mean to you? Although ecological awareness is hard to measure, you probably are much more aware of environmental concerns than your parents and their parents were when they were your age. Words like *ecology* and *recycling*—pretty much unheard of 40 years ago—are commonplace terms today.

People use products from Earth known as natural resources. Some of these resources are nonrenewable, which means they can't be produced in your lifetime. Others are known as renewable, which means we can replenish our supply of them. Because our life on Earth can become unstable if any natural resources disappear, it's important to learn how to conserve and protect the nonrenewable resources you'll discover in this unit.

Soil, forests, minerals, fossil fuels, water, and air are the resources you're going to examine in this unit. You'll look at models of different Earth systems to predict what may happen if people don't use them wisely. To continue our journey on spaceship Earth, all of us must share in protecting and conserving them for the future. One thing we can do is contribute to a composting project. To see how compost is made, do the Try This Activity on the next page.

Everyone, no matter where he or she lives, has the responsibility to respond to the challenge of preserving the stability of Earth for the generations to come. Let's see what that's all about!

Helping Earth Make New Soil

While you're studying this unit, make a compost pile. It takes a couple of months for things such as grass clippings, shredded branches, leaves, and vegetable scraps to turn into rich compost. But it doesn't take much work.

What You Need
trash can with lid
fruit and vegetable scraps, raw or cooked
high-nitrogen fertilizer
bulky plant materials
Activity Log **page 2**

1. With your classmates and teacher, decide on a place for your compost pile. You'll need an outside space at least 2 m (about 6.5 feet) on a side. Or you can use a large container such as a big trash can. (If you use a can or bag, punch 20 or 30 holes in it. Compost needs good air circulation.) If you use an open space instead, you may want to surround it with a fence of chicken wire so the compost materials don't blow away.

2. Collect fruit and vegetable scraps from your neighbors and bring them to school. Fruit and vegetable scraps are things like orange rinds, lemon rinds, apple cores, banana peels, potato peels, pumpkin shells, and nutshells. Your fruit and vegetable scraps can be cooked or raw, but be sure they don't contain any grease. (Grease might attract rats.) You can also collect vegetable trimmings and old vegetables discarded from grocery stores, if you ask at the produce department. Other things to bring from home are used tea bags, eggshells, and used coffee grounds with their coffee filters.

3. The other main ingredient for compost is lots of bulky, lightweight, plant materials such as dry leaves, shredded branches, sawdust, and grass clippings. You can even use old newspapers if you shred them.

4. To speed up the composting process, add a cupful of high-nitrogen fertilizer to the pile. Mix it in well.

5. Pile your compost materials into a high pile. If you're using a garbage can or trash bag, just fill it up! After a few days, it should be hot to the touch when you reach into the center of the pile. If your compost pile dries out, sprinkle it with water. (If there's a lot of rain, cover the pile with an old shower curtain so the rain doesn't wash everything away.

6. About every 2 weeks, turn the pile over with a rake. The materials that were on the outside need to move to the center so they'll decay and turn into compost. You can roll the trash can around to mix the contents, but be sure the lid stays on.

How have the materials changed from when you first placed them into the pile? Record your observations in your *Activity Log*. Note how each item looked before and after you composted it. How can you use compost?

Science in Literature

In these books, you'll find people like you and people different from you all trying to help Earth recover its balance and stability. Whether the book is fiction or nonfiction, it's bound to be full of ideas for doing the least possible harm and the most possible help in many areas of human behavior. Are you cooking? Boating? Building? Cleaning? There are ways to look at what you're doing to see how it affects Earth's systems. There are ways to keep your activities happy and fun but still consider Earth's needs.

50 Simple Things Kids Can Do to Save the Earth

by The Earthworks Group. Kansas City: Andrews and McMeel, A Universal Press Syndicate Company, 1990.

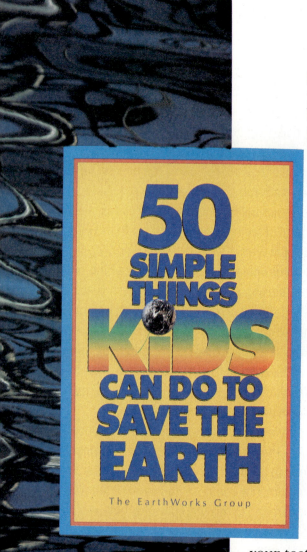

What can you yourself do to save Earth's natural resources? Lots of things. Cleaning up litter on a beach and snipping plastic pop-can loops, turning off the water while you brush your teeth, using a flea comb on your pet instead of chemical flea sprays, writing letters to the newspaper or elected officials about pollution and conservation, making a birdhouse from an old milk carton—these are just some of the 50 projects in this book. Also included are seven eco-experiments such as making recycled paper and testing the biodegradability of garbage. Each project includes the scientific details needed to understand why the project will help Earth.

Hatchet

by Gary Paulsen. New York: Bradbury, 1987.

This gripping novel tells the story of a thirteen-year-old boy's struggles to survive alone in northern Canadian after a plane crash. Brian is a city boy with no wilderness skills or supplies except a hatchet his mother gave him, which he almost didn't bring along. How would you use the natural resources of a northern lake and forest to keep yourself alive for months? Read this book to see how Brian learns to see clearly and think fast.

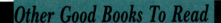

Other Good Books To Read

Cochrane, Jennifer. *Land Ecology.* **New York: The Bookwright Press, 1987.**

Learn how the land is structured and what makes it change. How can humans help the land support a good variety of life and increase its fertility? What kinds of soil accompany what kinds of ecology?

Ceremony—in the Circle of Life **by White Deer of Autumn. Milwaukee, Wisconsin: Raintree Publishers Inc., 1983.**

With beautiful watercolor illustrations by Daniel San Souci, this fiction book tells how Little Turtle, a nine-year-old Native American boy, was visited by Star Spirit and introduced to traditional teachings and ceremonies. Little Turtle learns to see all the world—including the animals and plants—as a community of brothers and sisters.

Going Green: A Kid's Handbook to Saving the Planet **by John Elkington** *et al.* **Harmondsworth, Middlesex, England: Viking, 1990.**

An Earth-minded attitude is possible about every habit from fixing your hair to changing a light bulb. Along with dozens of techniques for modifying your activities to make them resource-conservative, *Going Green* includes success stories about students whose ecological work has made headlines.

All these items help to maintain the stability of life on Earth.

How Do Soil and Forests Maintain Life on Earth?

***T*hink about the dirt beneath your feet. It's responsible for many resources on Earth. Let's find out how soil is the basis for the stability of all life on Earth.**

Minds On! Picture yourself as an animal such as an earthworm, mole, or groundhog living in the soil. What do you need from the soil in order to live? How does the moisture, dryness, hardness, or softness of the soil affect you? Now think about what soil provides for plants to exist. List your ideas. Look at your ideas of how an underground animal depends upon soil. What are the similarities? The differences? Write your ideas in your *Activity Log* page 3. ●

Earth's soil provides substances that enable living things to survive. All animals depend upon soil for food. Plants, in some way, are food for all animals. Animals eat plants or feed on animals that eat plants, or both.

To support life on Earth and maintain the stability of Earth's systems, soil is a valuable resource. In this lesson, you'll discover the uses of soil and how it supports plant life.

Soil aids plants by delivering water to their roots. What would happen if the soil were very hard and compact? Do the following Explore Activity to find out.

Activity!

Which Soil Allows Water To Flow Through Fastest?

Have you ever noticed places near your home or school where plants don't grow very well? Why do you think this is so? The reasons may be related to the quality of the soil or perhaps to the way it does or doesn't retain moisture. In this activity you'll explore factors that affect soil moisture.

What You Need

2 large coffee cans, open at both ends
beaker
water
trowel
small wooden board
hammer
metric ruler
masking tape
watch with second hand
Activity Log pages 4-5

What To Do

1 Find a place in the schoolyard or lawn where plants don't grow very well. Find another spot where the grass is thick and green. Use the trowel to remove a small section of sod from the grassy spot. Try to poke your pencil into the soil at each spot. Which soil seems harder? Describe any differences in appearance in your *Activity Log*.

Safety!

14

See the *Safety Tip* in step 2.

2 Using tape, mark the outside of each coffee can 5 cm from one end. Place a can at each location. Put the board on top of each can and have one person hold the board while another person hammers on the wood to push the can into the soil down to the 5-cm mark. *Safety Tip:* Use the hammer carefully. Keep your hands and fingers out of the way.

3 Pour 1 beaker of water into each can, and time how long it takes the water to soak into the ground. Record the soaking time at each location.

4 Make a graph to compare the soaking times for each location.

What Happened?

1. At which location was water absorbed more quickly? Explain why.
2. Remember the results when you poked the soil at each spot with your pencil. Do you think there is a relationship between soil hardness and soaking rate? Explain.

What Now?

1. Explain the relationship between your findings and the growth (or lack of growth) of plants at the soil locations.
2. How might you get grass to grow better on bare spots where little grass grows?

Soil Formation

In the Explore Activity, you were testing the **permeability** (pûr′mē ə bil′ i tē) of soil, or the ability of fluids to flow through soil. What characteristics allow fluids such as water to flow through the soil?

Minds On! Think about the soil you used in the Explore Activity or the soil you've seen in a park or near your home. What have you noticed about soil? Was it hard, soft, wet, or dry? Make a list of the various objects you've seen in soil. How do they affect the soil? List this information in your *Activity Log* on page 6. ●

Humans are dependent upon soil.

Soil is a mixture of rock, organic material, water, and air found on Earth's surface. Soil formation depends basically upon the five factors shown in the chart.

Soil takes an extremely long time to form. It can take up to 300 years for one centimeter (about one-half inch) of soil to form in some areas of the world.

When does soil formation begin? Soil formation begins when forces wear down rocks near Earth's surface.

There are two ways in which rock material begins to weather, or

Weathering by wind and water

Weathering by ice and water

Weathering by water

Time

Rock Type

Climate

Slope of Land

Plants and Animals

break down to become soil. It may start with physical weathering. During the process of **physical weathering,** rocks are broken into smaller pieces by such forces as wind, rain, and ice. Products of physical weathering range in size from large boulders to sand and clay-sized particles. A second type of weathering is chemical weathering. In **chemical weathering,** a rock's chemical composition is changed. New chemical compounds formed are used as nutrients for plants or can recombine with other elements in the soil.

Climate, too, affects how soil forms. How? Think about a cool, dry climate. Soil there forms more slowly because less chemical weathering takes place. Now think about a warm, moist climate. Soil there forms more quickly because there is more physical and chemical weathering.

The slope of the land has a great effect on formation of soil. If land has a flat surface, a deep layer of soil can form because water may not be able to run off the flat surface. Therefore, soil-making materials are not carried away by the water. Sloping land allows water to flow quickly, thereby carrying soil and rock particles away.

Organisms, both plant and animal, living in the soil aid soil development in several ways. When organisms die and decompose, organic material is formed. This organic material is called **humus.** Humus mixes with rock particles and forms soil.

Plants and animals also aid soil development by tunneling through the soil, making it more permeable. Plant roots even grow into cracks of rocks, wedge them apart, and assist in the process of weathering. How do you think they can do this? To test a plant's strength, do the Try This Activity below.

Earthworms aid in the development of soil.

Activity!

How Strong Are Plant Tissues?

Discover how strong plants can be!

What You Need

bean seeds, water, 2 35-mm film containers, plastic wrap, 2 rubber bands, *Activity Log* page 7

Fill both containers with as many bean seeds as they'll hold, then fill one container to the top with water. Cover both containers with plastic wrap and secure with rubber bands. What do you think will happen to each container overnight? Write your prediction in your *Activity Log.* Observe the containers the next day. What happened? Explain your observations in your *Activity Log.*

Nature's Earth Movers

Just as the bean seeds were able to swell and poke through the plastic, plants grow and wedge rocks and soil apart. Not only do plants have the ability to wedge rocks and soil as you've just determined, but animals can also move soil and rocks. One animal that provides an important service to soil is the earthworm. By tunneling through the soil, earthworms **aerate**—provide pockets of air—the soil and provide space for the entrance of air and water that cause further weathering. Earthworm tunnels serve as underground highways for many animals. Beneath every acre of grassland, there may live as many as a million earthworms, breaking down many tons of soil on Earth's surface. Moles and other burrowers such as shrews, beetles, and ground squirrels also help mix soil as they tunnel in all directions.

Did you know that there are thousands of kinds of soil on Earth? Soils can be black, red, brown, gray, yellow, and combinations of these colors. The soil's color depends upon its chemical composition. What the soil contains and the size and color of the particles in the soil are characteristics that determine the soil type. To investigate different characteristics of soil types, do the following activity.

Prairie dogs can make severe changes to land surfaces and soil.

TRY THIS

Activity!

How Different Are Soil Types?

What differences can you discover among various types of soil?

What You Need
soil samples
hand lens
Activity Log page 8

Examine each soil type. Look at its texture, color, compactness, and any objects contained in it. Describe each characteristic for each type of soil in your **Activity Log**. Are there many differences among the soil types? Discuss your findings with the class.

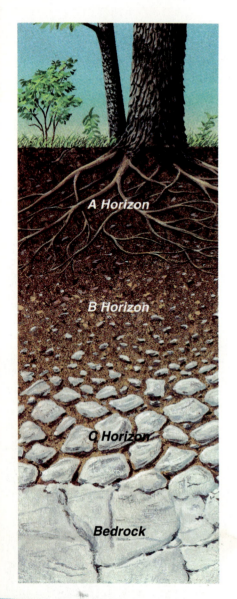

A Horizon

B Horizon

C Horizon

Bedrock

All types of soils eventually form layers called **soil horizons.** They can be thick or thin, and they can resemble the surrounding horizons or be very different from them. Boundaries between horizons can be distinct or hardly noticeable.

When water **percolates,** or filters downward through the soil horizons, it carries dissolved minerals down into lower horizons in a process known as **leaching.** Particles from upper layers of the soil are carried by the water into lower layers. Leaching assists in forming the different layers, making a soil profile.

A soil profile is a vertical section of all of the horizons that make up the soil. The topmost layer is known as the A horizon or topsoil. Organic matter, roots, and organisms like earthworms and insects are found in this layer. This horizon is well aerated and contains humus.

The next layer is known as the B horizon. This horizon often appears lighter in color and has fewer organisms than the A horizon. Some plant roots extend into this layer. Iron oxides and other materials leached from the A horizon are found in the B horizon.

The layer beneath the B horizon is the C horizon. It contains mostly weathered material from the surrounding rock. Below the C horizon is unweathered bedrock, from which soil can form.

The same forces such as wind, water, and ice that weather rock material can also erode the soil. **Soil erosion** is the transport of soil materials by wind, water, and ice. Will all of Earth's soil eventually be eroded into rivers and oceans? Once soil is eroded from one area, it is eventually deposited in another area. Where is soil transported? Soil and rock particles in the Rocky Mountains are carried by streams flowing down the mountain sides. These streams eventually flow into larger rivers such as the Mississippi or Colorado Rivers. Finally, the eroded soil and rock particles are carried into the oceans.

This process can also remove rich soils from one farmland and deposit them on another. Ancient Egyptian farmers relied heavily upon the Nile's yearly floods to bring rich, new deposits to their fields. These deposits added nutrients to the soil for farming. Areas such as the Great Sand Hills of Nebraska contain sands that were deposited there. Today, alfalfa and corn are grown in this soil.

Some people know a great deal about how erosion and deposition affect soil. One such person is a cooperative extension agent.

The Great Sand Hills in Nebraska

The Nile River in Egypt

21

Cooperative Extension Service Agent

Working to prevent soil erosion is just one of the duties that cooperative extension service agents have. These people are experts employed by both state and county governments to offer practical advice to the general public on a wide range of topics.

These specialists, usually associated with state agricultural colleges, are a source of current information ranging from conservation to farm management. Extension service specialists keep the public informed through newsletters and programs. Besides working with farmers on how to grow better-quality produce and control diseases, extension agents also collect soil samples to monitor the quality of the soil and test for nutrient deficiencies.

If you're interested in a career as a state or county extension agent, you must earn a bachelor of science degree from a college with an agricultural extension service or related program. As agricultural technology becomes more and more complicated, cooperative extension service agents will be needed to explain current research not just to farmers, but also to suburban gardeners and landscapers.

Because people depend heavily upon soil for almost everything they eat, soil stability is important. People such as cooperative extension service agents work to keep the soil from being eroded within an area. If there were no soil, no plants could grow. Soil stability enables plants to establish themselves and grow in a balanced system such as a forest.

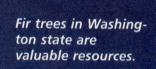

Fir trees in Washington state are valuable resources.

Our Diminishing Forests

A forest is a large area of land covered with trees. However, a forest is much more than just trees. There are many kinds of plants in a forest. How many different kinds can you name? The trees make it possible for these other kinds of plants to grow. Forests provide food and shelter for many different animals, too.

Forests are important to people for many reasons. Prehistoric people lived in the forest and obtained food there. Today, forests are one of Earth's riches due to their economic value, their environmental value, and the recreational area they provide.

The products people obtain from forests are lumber, paper, plastics, latex for making rubber, oils, waxes, and clothing fibers such as rayon. Many of these products are produced directly from specific forests, and others are manufactured by-products from trees.

Grove of Aspen trees in Arizona

How do you think forests are valuable to the environment? The soil within the forest is usually permeable and is able to absorb water to help prevent erosion and water runoff. The plants living in forests help to keep the oxygen and carbon dioxide in balance in Earth's atmosphere. This balance is essential for all life on Earth.

In many parts of the world, there are vast areas of forest land with dense forests and very few people nearby. Learn how to survive in a forest by reading the Literature Link on the following page.

Hatchet

In Gary Paulsen's novel *Hatchet,* thirteen-year-old Brian was the only survivor of a plane crash in northern Canada. Injured and ignorant of the wilderness, Brian knew he had to find food. He headed into the forest

"The trees were full of birds singing ahead of him in the sun.... He watched them fly, their color a bright slash in solid green, and in this way he found the berries...."

How would you go about surviving in a forest? With a group of classmates, list things you would need to find or make. Combine your list with those of other groups. Choose one thing from the combined lists and do research to learn how to make it. Try making and using it. Draw and write directions for making and using your small group's project, and keep the directions in a classroom Forest Survival Notebook.

Forests used to cover about 60 percent of Earth's land areas. Today, forests occupy roughly 30 percent of the land. What has happened?

Forests are being cleared for farmland, for their products, and to provide land for building cities. The destruction of forests is known as **deforestation.** Because people are cutting down forests, the stability of some of Earth's systems is being affected. Plants within forests make their food through the process of photosynthesis. Animals rely upon the trees to produce oxygen and absorb carbon dioxide. With fewer trees, less oxygen is being released into the air. Also, the fewer trees there are, the more carbon dioxide there is in the air, since trees remove this gas

from Earth's atmosphere in the process of making food.

People all over the world are concerned about deforestation. For example, the Gogol-Naru people of Papua, New Guinea, banded together to help save forests in their area.

A large lumber company cut down several thousand hectares of tropical rain forest in New Guinea, and in return the people in the area were promised better roads and social services. These benefits were never received by the Gogol-Naru people, even though their lands were leveled.

Gogol-Naru people

The Gogol-Naru people decided to take action. Petitions were signed and logging operations were temporarily halted. Negotiations continue today between the lumber company and the Gogol-Naru people regarding compensation for the lost forests and land.

Deforested lands in Brazil.

In Kenya, women have gathered together to start a tree-planting project. Approximately 50,000 women have helped to plant 10 million trees. Many valuable products are obtained from such forest lands. Many people benefit from the use of wood, lumber, and rubber by-products that forest land provides. Paper products are used every day by millions of people. To make all this paper, forests must be cut. How can our need for wood products be met without destroying Earth's forest? There's a delicate balance between proper use of Earth's resources and destructive overuse.

Landfills: Filling Up

Instead of simply dumping our garbage on unoccupied land, nowadays we dig trenches and bury garbage in landfills. This clears the land of trees and bushes and affects the soil that is used to bury the garbage.

Scientists known as garbologists study landfills to understand the composition and long-term fate of tons of buried debris. One reason scientists are interested in landfills is that 6,000 active landfills in the United States are reaching their capacity. In addition, the nation's trash bill is over $15,000,000,000 a year. As the number of operating landfills shrinks, scientists want to know what we're throwing out so decisions can be made about how to manage it in the future.

In 1991, every person in the United States generated almost two kilograms (about four pounds) of trash each day. One surprise was the discovery of the amount of paper people throw away. Newspaper is the largest item in landfills, taking up 18 percent of the space. Newspapers don't **biodegrade**—decay naturally—as people once thought. Newspapers have been found 40 years after being dumped and the headlines and articles could still be read!

When garbage is placed in a landfill, it's compacted and covered with 15 centimeters (6 inches) of soil. The garbage is eventually covered with 50 centimeters (20 inches) of soil to stop the percolation of water and keep the groundwater unpolluted. Normally, garbage biodegrades when it's in contact with the proper amount of air and water. Garbologists have found, though, that by sealing it from air or moisture, many landfills have been preserving garbage.

Sanitary landfill

Studies have shown that nine percent of garbage thrown out by people is edible food. If each household wasted less food, the decrease in refuse could be seen instantly. To get an idea of the amount of trash generated by one city in one day, do the Math Link.

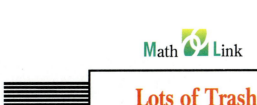

Math **Link**

Lots of Trash

A jumbo jet with a full load of people has a mass of about 348,750 kilograms (about 775,000 pounds). You just learned that in 1991 every person in the United States generated about 2 kilograms (about 4 pounds) of trash per day.

On average, how much trash does the city of St. Louis, Missouri, with a population of about 450,000, generate in one day? How many fully-loaded jumbo jets are equal in mass to that amount of trash?

Sum It Up

People all over the world rely upon soils and forests to provide them with products that they use every day. You examined soils and thought about how to protect forests in this lesson. The future of Earth's soils and forests depends upon you. Using these resources responsibly will allow you to preserve them for future generations. By planning now, you can prevent many problems such as filled-up landfills, deforestation, and soil erosion. The availability of soils, land, and forests are vital for your survival and the survival of your children. Only by attending to the needs of our forests and soils can we maintain the balance of Earth's natural resources.

Critical Thinking

1. Clay-sized particles are smaller than sand-sized materials. Which soil—sandy soil or clay—would be less permeable? Why?

2. Which type of weathering would occur if a highly fractured or cracked rock body were exposed to alternate freezing and thawing of water? Why?

3. How would the amount of humus in soil formed in the desert compare with the amount of humus formed in the same amount of time in a tropical climate?

4. Would you expect the A horizon or the B horizon in the same soil to be more weathered? Explain.

5. Explain how a pair of leather shoes can be traced back to the soil.

The materials used to build these items all came from Earth.

A Storehouse for Mineral Wealth and Energy Resources

What resources are found in Earth's crust? How do people use them? Minerals and fossil fuels are used every day by nearly everyone. How long will they last?

Have you ever realized that almost everything comes from Earth? Think about your cotton blue jeans, the bricks that make up your home, a hammer, a pair of eyeglasses, a wooden rocking chair—nearly anything you can think of (except maybe a meteorite from outer space) comes from Earth.

Minds On! Think about what materials are used to make a house or apartment. Make a chart in your *Activity Log* on page 9 that lists many building materials used and their sources. Where do these materials come from originally? ●

Many of the products in your home are made from natural resources. Glass is made from the mineral quartz. Steel is a mixture of iron and carbon. Quartz, iron, and carbon are only a few of the hundreds of substances found in Earth's crust. How do we obtain such resources from Earth's crust?

Activity!

How Are Mineral Deposits Located?

How difficult is the process of locating mineral deposits? What problems do people encounter when trying to mine the minerals? In the activity on these two pages, you'll explore a model of a mining problem, and you'll learn about the problems associated with first locating deposits and later restoring mining sites to their original states.

What You Need

Two-layer peanut butter, banana, and raisin bread sandwich
clear plastic straw
round toothpick
plastic knife
paper towel
Activity Log pages 10-11

What To Do

1 Set up your bookkeeping ledger on the *Activity Log* page. Your team has beginning capital of $500,000. Look over the lists of costs associated with locating deposits, mining, and restoring the area to its original condition. Refer to the selling prices to see how much your mined deposits are worth. Keep accurate records. You must purchase mineral rights to begin.

SELLING PRICE	
1 Gold deposit	$100,000
1 Molybdenite deposit	$350,000

MINING COSTS	
Mineral rights	$10,000
Surface deposit removal	$15,000
Core sample	$10,000
Whole layer removal	$100,000

RESTORATION COSTS	
Restoration of whole layer	$20,000
Filling area of gold deposit	$70,000
Filling area of molybdenite deposit	$70,000
Unrestored Area	$100,000

30

2 Place your "mineral lease area" (sandwich) on the paper towel. Pretend the sandwich is land and the raisins are outcrops of gold ore. The "hidden" banana slices are larger deposits of molybdenite. The metal molybdenum is made from this ore. It is added to steel to make it resistant to high temperatures.

3 Before you mine each layer, make a drawing of the area in your *Activity Log.* You will need to refer to your drawings to restore the site.

4 "Surface deposits" can be mined with the tooth pick. Hidden ore deposits may be located by examining "drill cores." A "drill core" can be made by pushing the plastic straw through the mineral area. Remove the straw and examine your core sample. Earth layers can be removed to reach underground deposits. Remember your budget is limited and you must restore the area to its original condition.

5 Record in your *Activity Log* the total number of deposits you found. Share your data with the class to make two graphs—one showing the number of surface deposits and the other the total number of deposits mined.

What Happened?

1. Compare the number of surface deposits with the total number of deposits mined. Calculate the percentage of total deposits represented by those found at the surface. How does this compare to the percentage of "deep" deposits?

2. Describe the financial condition of your "mining company."

What Now?

1. Tell how you decided how many core samples to purchase and how you decided the location of each sample.

2. Explain why it is more expensive to mine deeply hidden deposits than those located at the surface.

3. How easy was it to put the land back the way it was before you began mining? Compare this to restoring a mining site to its original condition after mining operations are completed.

EXPLORE

Minerals—
Part of Earth's Crust

The pigments used to color this paint are from minerals.

Natural resources are not spread evenly over the world, just as the bananas were not throughout your sandwich. Minerals are one type of natural resource. A **mineral** is a naturally occurring, inorganic (that is, not formed from organisms) solid with a definite internal structure based upon its arrangement of atoms and molecules.

Minds On! Make a list of several natural resources in your *Activity Log* on page 12. Now, place a check mark by each item that you'd consider to be a mineral. How are minerals different from the other natural resources on your list? ●

It has been known for thousands of years how useful minerals are. Stone Age people used minerals for tools and jewelry. If you use talcum powder after a bath, pencils at school, or salt on your food, you are using minerals. The quartz crystals in most watches are also minerals. Most modern paints include mineral pigments for coloring, and rocks such as chalk and clay provide minerals that thicken paint.

Geologists have identified over 3,000 minerals! They conduct research to find new uses for the minerals that have been identified. Minerals such as

Minerals are often extracted from Earth by strip mining.

copper, gold, and silver are called **metallic minerals,** because they are a source of metals. Other minerals, such as quartz, diamonds, and sulfur, are **non-metallic minerals**—they don't yield metals. A **rock** is composed of one or more minerals.

Today, many rocks and minerals are used in construction. The outsides of some buildings are made of granite or sandstone. Elements such as iron, aluminum, copper, and tin are extracted from certain minerals and used to make beams and wiring.

How do we know so much about minerals? Scientists known as mineralogists study them to obtain information about each mineral.

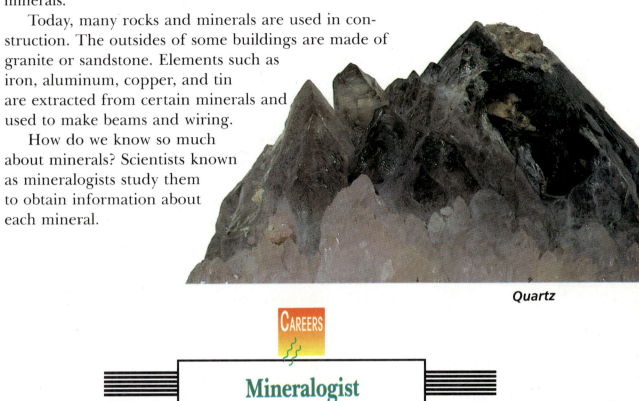

Quartz

CAREERS

Mineralogist

Mineralogists identify minerals and conduct research to find ways for people to use them. They study the structure of minerals to see what the crystal structure is inside the mineral.

Another duty of a mineralogist is to classify minerals and study their characteristics. This is done with the use of microscopes and X-ray refractometers—instruments that look inside the mineral and photograph the internal structure. Mineralogists also study physical properties of minerals such as hardness, color, luster, and conductivity.

To become a mineralogist you need a bachelor's degree in geology or a related field of earth science and a master's degree in mineralogy. In this field, you'd be employed by companies to conduct research on mineral deposits or even help locate various deposits around the world. Universities employ mineralogists to teach geology and other earth science classes. Any position, whether it is in private business, government, or education, would probably require conducting research.

Trading beads were made from Earth's materials.

Rocks and minerals that are found in quantities large enough to make them worth mining are called **ores.** Ores have been mined for thousands of years. For example, ancient Egyptians mined emeralds to use for jewelry. They also used the process of electroplating to coat jewelry with a thin layer of gold. How exactly are gold deposits mined from Earth's crust?

Think back to your model of mining in the Explore Activity. How might this compare to methods of gold mining that are used today? Gold-bearing rocks are usually found in sand and gravel deposits near river beds. Sand and gravels are deposited by streams or rivers in areas where the velocity of the water decreases. When the river current slows, it can't carry as much sediment as when it was moving quickly. As the current slows, sand and gravel settle to the bottom.

One method of gold mining is known as placer mining. It works by separating the dense gold from other substances that aren't as dense. Placer mining is the oldest method of gold mining. How exactly does it work? Miners fill a pan with water and place handfuls of dirt and sand into the pan. The pan is then swirled, and the dense materials settle in the center of the pan.

Drills and arrowheads were made from minerals and rocks.

Placer mining

34

Energy Resources

Diamonds and iron, both inorganic materials, are natural resources used for their economic value. Other natural resources, such as fossil fuels, are organic material. **Fossil fuels,** mined for their energy value, are substances formed from organisms that lived on Earth millions of years ago. Coal, oil, and natural gas are fossil fuels.

The sun supplies energy for many Earth processes and enables plants and animals to live and grow. Often, when these organisms die, they become buried by loose Earth materials called sediments. As the remains of organisms decay and become compressed by the mass of overlying sediments, all the water is squeezed from them. Over millions of years, pressure and heat turn the organic material into fossil fuels. Most organisms are made up of hydrogen and carbon. When they die and their bodies are subjected to heat and pressure by overlying sediments, the elements hydrogen and carbon remain. Therefore, fossil fuels contain hydrogen and carbon and are known as **hydrocarbons.**

Coal was used for fuel as early as 3,000 to 4,000 years ago in the country of Wales. As early as the 12th century, the Hopi Indians mined coal by scraping and digging. They used it for cooking and in ceremonial chambers.

How do you think people use coal today? Approximately 23 percent of the electrical energy in the United States is supplied by coal. We obtain coal by mining it from Earth's surface or from underground mines. Mining near Earth's surface is called **strip mining** because layers of soil and rock overlying the deposits are stripped away.

Coal was used as fuel for steam engines.

Major coal deposits in the United States

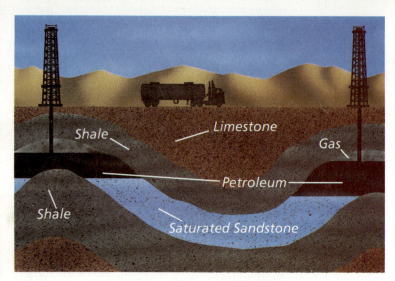

Shale

Limestone

Gas

Petroleum

Shale

Saturated Sandstone

*Petroleum is a liquid formed from microorganisms that lived millions of years ago. This oil then became trapped in porous rock such as sandstones and limestones. In places where vast amounts of oil became trapped, **oil reservoirs** were formed. These reservoirs are drilled today for oil and natural gas.*

Egyptian mummy

In strip mining, cuts are made side by side and trenches are dug to reach the coal seam. Then, small mechanical shovels are used to dig out the coal. As each new trench is excavated, the material that is dug out is dumped into an old trench.

In some places, the coal can't be reached directly from the surface. A gently sloping entry shaft, known as a slope mine, is then used to reach coal seams that are within a few hundred meters of the surface.

When coal seams are far beneath the surface, a vertical shaft mine is dug. This type is difficult to build and operate. Why do you think this is so? (Recall the model mining activity you performed with the sandwich.)

Another fossil fuel, petroleum, was used by many ancient civilizations. The ancient Egyptians used it to help preserve mummies. Our word *mummy* comes from the Persian word *mum,* meaning a type of tar. The ancient Chinese used petroleum to heat and light their homes and to cook. Tar pits supplied crude oil that was used for fuel, cooking, and lighting in ancient Latin America. At the same time, petroleum was used in Europe for lubricating wagon wheels and in ointments that stopped swelling and helped cuts heal. We still use petroleum products today for some of these purposes.

Another type of fossil fuel is **natural gas,** also a hydrocarbon. Natural gas is usually found in oil reservoirs above the surface of the oil. It's not as dense as liquid petroleum, and it rises above the petroleum within the reservoir.

Our use of fossil fuels has changed throughout history. Coal was the main source of fuel in 1900, but as inventions changed from steam-driven to petroleum-driven, petroleum products overtook coal as the main fuel. Today, petroleum is still the most widely used fossil fuel.

Ever since 1900, energy consumption has doubled approximately every 20 years. Because of the use of such large amounts of fossil fuels, the sources are running out. They are nonrenewable, which means they can't be replaced. To see how much energy you may use with just one appliance, read the Literature Link.

Burning natural gas supplies heat for cooking.

Literature  Link

50 Simple Things Kids Can Do To Save the Earth

... Did You Know

● We open our refrigerators almost 22 times a day. That's over 8,000 times a year for each one of us!

● When you open the refrigerator, the cold air you feel coming out is trading places with hot air going in. That means the fridge is getting warmer inside, and has to use lots of extra electricity to cool back down.

... What You Can Do

● Don't open your refrigerator unless you have to. Once you've opened it, quickly get what you want and close the door. Think about what you want *before* you open it.

... See For Yourself

● Keep a record of how many times you open the refrigerator during the day. Are you opening it more than you really need to? And how long do you keep it open?

In *50 Simple Things Kids Can Do To Save the Earth* by The Earthworks Group appear many energy-saving tips. What advice can you give people to help them use energy more wisely? Brainstorm energy-wise tips. Decide how your group will present its tips—will you make a poster? Write a skit? Write and perform a rap or poem?

Effects on the Environment

Coal mining in Montana

People use minerals and fossil fuels every day. But the use of many minerals and fossil fuels harms the environment.

How can strip mining affect the surrounding environment? To see, do the Try This Activity.

Mining coal, especially in humid areas that receive a lot of rainfall, can pollute groundwater supplies. As you discovered in the activity, the pH of water coming into contact with sulphur coal is changed. You may not see the chemical change, but it's there. Sulfuric acid can form and wash into rivers and groundwater sources. This problem can be controlled by changing and directing the course of water flow near the mine. This can reduce pollution, erosion, and water treatment costs.

Strip mining in Oklahoma

Environmentalists have long opposed strip mining because of the damage it does to the landscape. Waste rock removed from the mine was once left in unsightly piles and heaps. Now, most states require strip mining operations to reclaim or restore the land. Environmental regulations require the waste rock to be replaced and then covered with topsoil. The land that was once stripped of its mineral resources may now be ready to grow crops, forests, or grassy fields.

By conserving energy, people will use less fossil fuel and the environment will be better. If you put your ideas to use, you can make a difference in improving the environment and decreasing your consumption of the declining supply of fossil fuels.

Activity!

How Does Coal Change Water?

Strip mining of sulfur coal can change ground water. How?

What You Need

hammer, towel, pieces of sulfur coal, container filled with hot water, pH paper, safety goggles, *Activity Log* page 13

Safety Tip: Be careful with the hammer, and keep your fingers away while crushing the coal. Be sure to wear safety goggles while using the hammer to crush the coal.

Wrap some coal in the towel and crush it with the hammer. Test the pH of the water in the container and record your observations in your *Activity Log.* Place pieces of coal into the container filled with water. Wait about 30 minutes and then retest the pH of the water sample. Record your observations in your *Activity Log.* How has the water changed?

Sum It Up

In modern times, people have become dependent upon the use of minerals and fossil fuels. Unfortunately, there are limited amounts of these natural resources. People's methods of obtaining these resources from Earth's crust have often left the land barren and the environment polluted. You determined in the Explore Activity that it's not always an easy job to reconstruct land that has been mined. However, it can be done. If people better understand the limited amounts of minerals and fossil fuels and work to conserve them, a balance can exist between the great demand for these resources and the diminishing supplies.

Critical Thinking

1. Why do you think some minerals are so valuable and others are not? Explain.

2. Explain how gold can be mined. Have the techniques changed over the years? Why or why not?

3. Explain how fossil fuels can be considered solar resources.

4. List ways in which lands that have been mined can be restored. Explain how your ideas can be accomplished.

5. List several ways that you and your family can conserve fossile fuels.

*Water is used in a
variety of ways.*

Would You Like a Glass of Water?

Water, water, everywhere—or is it? Have you ever wondered what would happen if Earth ran out of water?

Minds On! Think about how you depend on water for your daily activities. With three classmates, brainstorm a list of ways in which water is used. Are all of these activities necessary? Is water being used wisely? Record your ideas in your *Activity Log* on page 14. ●

We use water every day, and our demand for it is increasing. Now, it's more important than ever that we make better use of our supplies. In one sense, the supplies are limited—all the water we'll ever have is present on Earth now. Yet in another sense, supplies are unlimited—water goes through a cycle, and people keep reusing the water present on Earth. The more we learn about water, the more we'll be able to conserve it, protect it, and use it wisely.

Next to air, water is what is most urgently needed to keep us alive. The human body uses water to digest food, eliminate waste, and regulate its temperature. Your body is about 60 percent water. So is that of a mouse. An elephant and an ear of corn are about 70 percent water, a potato and an earthworm are about 80 percent water, and a tomato is almost 95 percent water.

An adult can live without food for two months, but can live without water for only a few days. You know that water is needed in order to support life and for use in daily activities. But how much water do you actually use?

Activity!

How Much Water Is Used at School?

Do you have any idea how much water is used at school each day? How can you find out? Think about the ways you use water at school.

What You Need

various containers
watch with a second hand
Activity Log **pages 15-16**

What To Do

1 As a class, make a list of ways water is used at school. Combine all lists to form a class list. Then form groups of four, each of which will be responsible for the data gathering and calculating for one kind of water use.

2 Determine ways to measure the amount of water used in each of the activities on your group's list, such as the amount of water used to water the lawn, to flush a toilet, to wash hands, and to get a drink from a drinking fountain.

3 Before you begin gathering your data, estimate how much water you think is used in each activity. Estimate how many times every day each use occurs.

4 Decide how to check your estimate; that is, how to determine how often these uses do occur in your school on an average day.

5 Design your experiment and gather data.

6 Share your measurements and calculations with the class. Build a class data table showing ways water is used and the daily amounts for each listed item.

7 Determine the total amount of water usage daily, weekly, and for the entire school year. Are some uses higher in certain seasons of the year?

What Happened?

1. How many liters of water did you estimate are used daily, weekly, and in one school year in each activity?
2. What problems did you encounter when gathering your data? How did you overcome them?
3. Which activities did you find consumed the most water? The least?

What Now?

1. What are some ways water could be conserved at school?
2. Estimate how many liters of water could be saved daily, weekly, or in one year at school with one of your suggestions.
3. Could any of those ways also work to conserve water at home? Explain.

EXPLORE

Earth Reuses Water

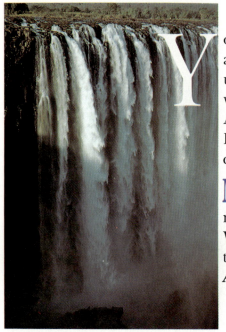

Victoria Falls on the Zambezi River

You may now know how much water is used every day at one school. Can you imagine how much water is used by the entire world? Not only do people use water, but every plant and animal must use water, too. And water has to be clean to be useable. Read the Literature Link on this page to see how you can help clean up your local waterways.

Minds On! If you try, you can think of many ways to conserve clean water. Design a plan to reuse one bucket of water as many times as possible. Write the ways you might reuse this water, along with the order in which the steps are to be done, in your *Activity Log* on page 17. ●

Literature  Link

50 Simple Things Kids Can Do To Save the Earth

... Did You Know
● The color and smell of a stream can tell you what's happening to it.
● **Muddy water:** Can mean there's too much dirt in the water, which makes it hard for fish to breathe. The stream may need more plants along its bank.
● **A shiny film on the water:** Can mean there's oil leaking into the stream. That's poison and should be stopped.

...What You Can Do
● Organize a party to plant trees along stream banks. This will keep the soil from washing away into the stream and protect animals that live in the stream as well.
● If you find anything like oil or sewage leaking into the water, report it to a parent or other adult.

In *50 Simple Things Kids Can Do To Save the Earth* by The Earthworks Group, these tips and others will help you conserve our waterways. Adopt a stream! Form a small group and use a map to study streams nearby. Plan to observe the sites. Look for pollution in water and on land, and plan to clean up any trash you may find. If possible, arrange a tree-planting project.

In the *Air, Weather, and Climate* unit, you discover the water cycle when you study how clouds and precipitation form. Rain leaves puddles in the streets and fields. Through the process of evaporation, the liquid water changes to a water vapor, a gas, and rises into the atmosphere. As water vapor rises, it cools, condenses, and may eventually fall back to Earth as precipitation. Precipitation usually falls as rain; if the air is cold enough, it falls as snow or sleet.

Water can also be absorbed by the roots of plants. Some of this absorbed water ends up in the air again because plants transpire. Did you know a birch tree gives off over 268 liters (about 70 gallons) of water a day, and corn gives off about 37,000 liters (about 4,000 gallons) per 0.5 hectare (about 1 acre) daily?

1. Energy from the sun causes water to evaporate into the air above it.

2. Transpiration is the process by which plants expel water vapor into the air.

3. As air cools, molecules of gases move closer together causing water vapor to condense. It falls back to Earth as precipitation such as rain or snow.

4. Precipitation that hasn't run off soaks into the ground and becomes part of the groundwater supply. **Groundwater** is water that flows beneath the surface through rocks and soil in the upper part of Earth's crust. **Runoff** is water that flows over the ground rather than soaking in.

The Water Cycle

Earth reuses its water in a global system called the water cycle.

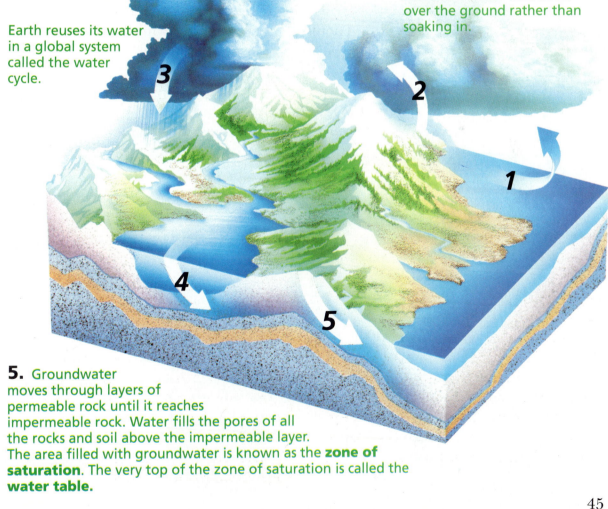

5. Groundwater moves through layers of permeable rock until it reaches impermeable rock. Water fills the pores of all the rocks and soil above the impermeable layer. The area filled with groundwater is known as the **zone of saturation**. The very top of the zone of saturation is called the **water table**.

Desalination is a simple process in which sea water is boiled and the steam is piped into a cool bottle. As evaporation occurs, the salt is left behind. The steam that cools in the bottle condenses into fresh water.

The water cycle is very stable and continues to circulate everywhere on Earth. If water is always going through a cycle, why should we worry about running out? After all, 70 percent of Earth's surface is covered by water. The problem is that most of this is not fresh water but salt water. Can we use salt water?

Much of the salt in sea water is halite, or common rock salt. A person can safely drink water that contains less than one-half kilogram (about one pound) of salt for every 100 kilograms (220 pounds) of water. But seawater has about seven times that amount of salt. Therefore, a person who drinks only sea water can't survive!

It's possible to change salt water into fresh water through a process called desalination, but the costs of both removing the salt and then getting the fresh water to the places where it's needed are great.

Seawater

Condensing fresh water

Evaporating fresh water

Boiling seawater

Fresh water

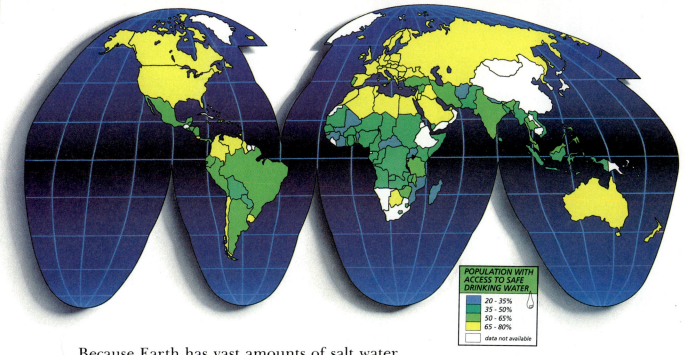

POPULATION WITH
ACCESS TO SAFE
DRINKING WATER

	20 - 35%
	35 - 50%
	50 - 65%
	65 - 80%
	data not available

Because Earth has vast amounts of salt water, desalination may soon be used more for obtaining fresh water. Natural sources of fresh water are limited. In addition, freshwater supplies are not evenly distributed across the globe. Some areas have plentiful supplies, while other areas have very little fresh water available.

Generally, the world's most heavily populated areas receive enough rain for their needs. These areas include most of Europe, southeast Asia, the eastern United States, India, China, and northwestern Asia. But about half of Earth's land masses don't receive enough rain. These dry areas include most of Asia, central Australia, most of northern Africa, and the Middle East.

Water isn't distributed evenly, either. For example, in the 1980s severe droughts baked the midwestern and southeastern United States, as well as parts of Argentina, Australia, Brazil, Ethiopia, Paraguay, and Uruguay. But during the same decade, floodwaters soaked the land in the south-central United States and parts of Bangladesh, China, and India.

The distribution of water has always been uneven, and people have had to adjust to varying water supplies. Today, in the western United States, people have made adjustments that have changed the Colorado River.

Ethiopian woman

Is the Colorado River a Natural or an Artificial Resource?

The Colorado River of today that flows from Colorado to Mexico scarcely resembles the Colorado River of 100 years ago. Today, some people refer to the 2,400 kilometers (1,440 miles) of the Colorado River as a network of concrete plumbing!

Because of the changes people have made, the river's appearance has been drastically altered. Some of the changes have helped the river. For example, at one time spring and summer flooding followed by erosion meant that very few plants grew near the Colorado River in the Grand Canyon. Now the flow of the river is regulated by the Glen Canyon Dam at the Utah-Arizona border. Without the flooding and erosion, it was possible to plant dense, woody vegetation from North Africa along the shores. Now that vegetation thrives!

But some species of water life have disappeared completely, and others are endangered as a direct result of building the Glen Canyon Dam. The water flowing in the Colorado River and into the Grand Canyon is drawn from 60 meters (about 200 feet)

The Grand Canyon at the Colorado River

below the surface of Lake Powell. The depth is so great that light can't penetrate and warm the water. The constant water temperature has caused trouble for the fish that normally begin their reproductive cycles when water temperatures rise. They've been unable to adapt to the colder river water.

People dammed the Colorado in order to divert water to surrounding areas. Each year there are more controversies—which communities need the water most? What damage may occur to the environment near the dams? Developers argue that the Southwest needs the water and also the electricity that the flowing river water generates. Environmentalists argue that the Grand Canyon's unique natural beauty must be protected.

Conduct research to learn about the communities that draw water from the Colorado River in both the United States and Mexico. How will future water and energy needs change the river even more? Investigate the issues that the altering of the river has raised. Then write a short essay in your *Activity Log* on page 18 evaluating the issues. Whose rights should come first? Try to think of a way to compromise so that all parties' needs are met.

Glen Canyon Dam

Lake Powell

The area near the mouth of the Colorado River

Much of the southwestern United States obtains its water from the Colorado River. Do you know the source for your drinking water? Water is taken from rivers, lakes, reservoirs, and wells. Much of this water isn't pure and must be treated before people can use it. To see how water can be cleaned, do the following activity.

In much the same way as you cleaned the muddy tap water with the use of sand and a paper filter, the water at water-treatment centers goes through certain processes in order to be cleaned. It's tested to see if it contains harmful bacteria, plants, or chemicals. Near the ocean, water may also be tested for traces of salt.

The water you drink everyday goes through cleaning processes before you receive it.

Activity!

How Can Water Be Cleaned?

Water carries sediment, debris, and pollutants. To be useful, it must be cleaned. Try cleaning some water.

What You Need

2-L soft-drink bottle with bottom cut out
cap for the bottle with a hole in it
filter paper
soil
sand to fill 1/3 of a 2-L bottle
4 containers
water
Activity Log page 19

Place a 2-L bottle upside down with the cap on over 1 container. Mix the soil with the tap water in the container until the water becomes muddy. Pour some of this muddy water into the 2-L bottle. In your *Activity Log*, first predict what will happen to the water. Describe the water as it flows out of the bottle. Save this water sample.

Next, place the 2-L bottle upside down with the cap on over another container. Line the bottom of the bottle with the paper filter. Pour some muddy water into the bottle. Again, predict what will happen to the water, and then describe the water after it has flowed through the bottle and filter.

Next, wash the 2-L bottle and place it upside-down with the cap on over a third container. Put the sand into the bottle. Pour some muddy water into the sand-filled bottle. In your *Activity Log*, predict what will happen to the water. Describe the water as it flows out of the bottle. Compare it to the water that passed through the filter paper. Which is cleaner? Why do you think this is so? How does this process clean the water? Write your observations in your *Activity Log*.

Another test detects acids that might corrode water pipes and injure people. If the acid level is too high, chemicals must be added to lower the acid level before the water is useable.

Water is usually treated with alum, or potassium and aluminum salts, to make the sediment in the water stick together and become heavy enough to sink to the bottom of the water tank.

Next, the water flows through layers of fine, clean sand, which filters out most small solids, just as the sand in your experiment filtered some sediment from the muddy water.

Sometimes air is sent bubbling through the water to improve the color and taste. To make sure no bacteria can survive in it, chlorine is added. Most cities also add fluoride, which helps prevent cavities in your teeth.

Language Arts  Link

Which Cities Use the Most Water?

Form groups of three, choose a part of the country, and do research to determine its water source. In your group, write a formal business letter and send it to the City Water Department of selected cities within your chosen part of the country. Ask for an estimate of that particular city's water use per year. On a national map, record your group's findings. Show which cities use the most water and which cities use the least. Try to explain the differences in your *Activity Log* on page 20.

Maintaining Clean Water Supplies

Water pollution is a large-scale problem. What are some sources of water pollution? Raw sewage pumped into rivers, lakes, and oceans pollutes many city water supplies. Fertilizers, pesticides, and insecticides that leach into groundwater supplies are common in farming regions. Liquid wastes from large manufacturing plants pumped into bodies of water, materials leached from landfills, and careless disposal of hazardous wastes are other common sources of water pollution. To test ways water can be polluted, do the following activity.

Activity!

What Happens to Water Flowing Through Contaminated Sediment?

Water that flows through sediment can pick up contaminants. Sometimes you can see the change in the water, and sometimes you can't. How do you know the water has changed if you can't see any difference?

What You Need

2 small milk cartons (each with a small hole in the bottom), colored tissue paper (shredded), soil or sand to fill the cartons, shredded lemon, orange, or tomato peels, pH paper, 2 containers, warm water, *Activity Log* page 21

To create a model of a landfill, fill 1 carton with alternating layers of sand or soil and shredded tissue paper. Use thick layers of tissue paper. Pour warm water into the carton until water begins to flow through the bottom of it into a container. Note the appearance of the water in your *Activity Log*. How has it changed?

Next, fill the second carton with alternating layers of soil and shredded fruit peels. Pour warm water through the carton so the water drains into the other container. Do you notice any change in the water's appearance? Test the pH of the water that has drained out. Now, test the water from the tap where you obtained your warm water. Note any differences in your *Activity Log*.

What happened to the water? Can you relate this activity to water flowing through a landfill? What have you proved about how landfills can affect groundwater supplies?

Antipollution efforts in the 1960s and 1970s resulted in declines in the levels of many toxic, or poisonous, substances in Lake Erie and other Great Lakes. The Cuyahoga River in Cleveland, Ohio, was so polluted in the summer of 1969 that the river caught fire and burned as a result of the chemicals in the water. The Great Lakes are now cleaner than they have been in years past. Some of the beaches have re-opened, and untreated sewage no longer flows into the lakes causing high levels of bacteria.

Water supplies can also be maintained through conservation. Think of all of the ways your family uses water. The average American uses more than 240 liters (about 64 gallons) of water a day in his or her home.

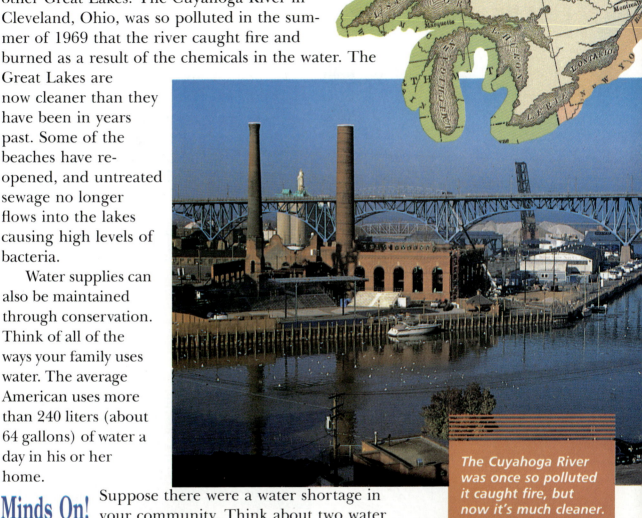

The Great Lakes

The Cuyahoga River was once so polluted it caught fire, but now it's much cleaner.

Minds On! Suppose there were a water shortage in your community. Think about two water conservation plans. The first plan should be one that your family can practice on a daily basis to conserve water. The second should be in case of severe water shortage. In what ways would you conserve water? In what ways would it be most difficult to apply water conservation procedures? Write your ideas in your *Activity Log* on page 22. ●

One way to conserve water would be not to water landscape plants. However, new methods of plant propagation and landscaping have been developed so that some plants use as little water as possible. Let's investigate these new methods.

The burning of the Cuyahoga River

Xeric Landscaping

Labels on landscape plan: NATIVE TREES · MULCH PATH · WOOD DECK · WILD-FLOWERS · RESIDENCE · GRAVEL · NATIVE GRASSES · DROUGHT-TOLERANT SOD · DRIVE · NATIVE GROUND COVER · NATIVE SHRUBS

Are there trees, flowers, or other plants around your home? What do these plants need to stay alive? Many liters of water are used every year to irrigate our landscapes. One new type of landscaping that conserves water is called xeric (zer´ ik) landscaping. *Xeric* comes from the Greek word *xeros,* which means "dry." Although it's most useful in arid lands, it can benefit any climate. The goal of xeric landscaping is to grow plants that need no watering.

Desert plants such as yuccas and cacti can do well anywhere, even in rainy climates, if planted on raised mounds spaced apart to allow room for their shallow, wide-ranging root systems. Heavy mulching—that is, placing thick layers of wood chips or other plant material around trees, shrubs, and vegetable gardens—is an important part of xeric landscaping. Mulching reduces evaporation of water from the soil surface. This keeps the plants cooler and allows them to use less water. Also, the mulch stops weed growth,

Xeric landscaping plans are used to landscape gardens and the areas around homes.

reduces soil compaction and erosion, and increases the soil's organic content.

Experts estimate that residential xeric landscaping adds 10 to 15 percent to property values and reduces maintenance costs and water bills by 30 to 60 percent. It also improves the appearance of the community and frees water supplies for drinking and other uses.

In times of drought, communities can lose millions of dollars worth of conventional landscape plants. But xeric landscape plants can withstand droughts because they either use very little water or go dormant during a drought, bouncing back when water returns.

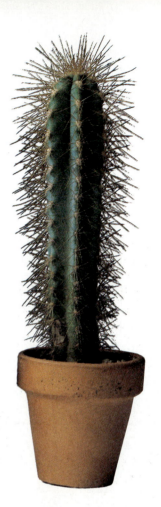

Cacti are often used in xeric landscaping.

Sum It Up

As you know, water is necessary for life on Earth. If everyone were to understand how to conserve water and use this knowledge, there would be plenty of clean fresh water for all because of the stability of Earth's water cycle. But if water conservation is not practiced, people will unbalance the water cycle, and our future will include polluted water or even no natural fresh water at all. You've discovered how water is used at school and how heavily we depend upon it. The next time you get a glass of water, think about what a valuable resource you're about to swallow.

Critical Thinking

1. Explain how clouds are important parts of Earth's water cycle.

2. How is Earth's water cycle powered?

3. Polar ice is a source of fresh water. What do you think is the biggest problem that could result if a chunk of polar ice were towed from Greenland to a drought-stricken area in Africa?

4. Would gravel or sand make a better filter for ground water? Explain.

5. In the early 1900s, Americans used about 379 liters of water per person per day. Today, the average amount of water used per person per day is 7,100 liters! What is the amount of increase in average water use? List three or more ways people use water now that accounts for the increase in average use.

Earth's air is used by everyone on Earth. All people's activities affect the cleanliness of Earth's air.

How About a Breath of Fresh Air?

What makes the air fresh? Do you
know what the air you're breathing contains?

Minds On! Imagine that a severe air-pollution alert
has just been issued for your community.
What do you think might have caused this air-pollution
alert? List your ideas in your *Activity Log* on page 23.
Compare your list with those of classmates. What are
some ways you could tell if the air were highly
polluted, even if you hadn't been informed of the
pollution alert? ●

If you've ever been in a polluted area, such as a
smoke-filled room, you've experienced what it's like to
breathe contaminated air. As often as you breathe
every day, you may want to be aware of the air you're
inhaling.

Math **Link**

How Much Air Do You Breathe?

Determine how many breaths you take in one
minute. Calculate how many times you breathe in one
hour, one day, and one year. Conduct research to find
the volume of air inhaled in one breath. Calculate the
volume of air you breathe in one year. According to
the average volume of air inhaled while you breathe,
calculate how many breaths of air it would take to fill
your classroom.

Once air becomes polluted, how can it be cleaned?
In this lesson, you'll discover what determines air quality, and examine some ways pollution can be controlled.

Activity!

What Pollutants Are in the Air?

There are several types of air pollution. How do we know exactly what they are and how they got there? Some pollutants such as ashes or soot are solids. Others are in the form of gases. To see some of the solids in the air around you, you'll be constructing devices for comparing amounts and types of particles in the air from day to day.

What You Need

scissors
3 round plastic lids with
    centers cut out
metric ruler
hole punch
string
transparent tape
hand lens
Activity Log pages 24-25

What To Do

1 Punch a hole near one edge of each plastic lid.

2 Cut 3 pieces of string, each long enough to hang the lids from various locations. Put a piece of string through the hole in each lid. Tie a loop in the string so that you can hang the lid by the string.

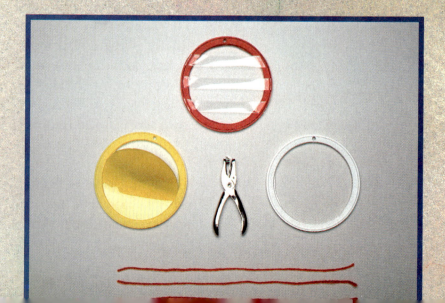

3 Place 3 strips of tape across the opening in each plastic lid, leaving space between the pieces of tape.

4 Find a different place to hang each lid. Choose some indoor locations and some outdoor locations. Be sure to hang the lids in areas where air circulates, such as near vents and air registers. Label each lid with a letter **A** through **C** and your name. Keep a list of where you hung each lid.

5 The next day, collect the lids. As you collect each one, don't breathe or blow on the lids. Use a hand lens to observe any particles that collected on the tape. Record your observations in your *Activity Log*.

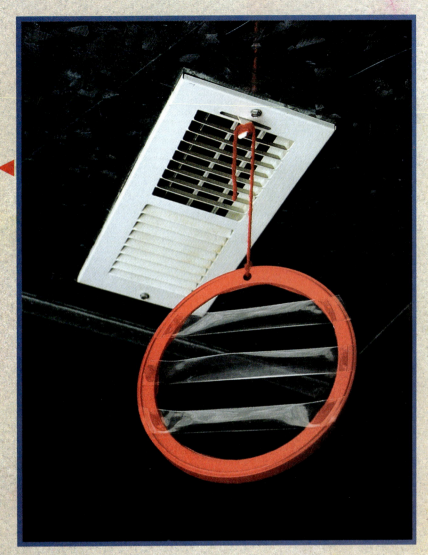

What Happened?

1. What did you observe on the tape?
2. Where did you find the most solid air pollutants? Why do you think this is so?
3. Which type of solid air pollutant occurred most often?

What Now?

1. What can you do to help reduce air pollution in these locations?
2. Would you expect to detect more or fewer pollutants on a windy day?
3. What types of pollution might your investigation not detect?

Air Quality

It's amazing how many solid particles are present in the air. The particles that you detected with your strips of tape in the Explore Activity are probably in the air everywhere in the world. Earth's air interacts with every other Earth system. The air circulates around the world resulting in everyone using the same air. Earth has maintained this system of circulating air for millions of years. However, people are altering this system by adding more substances to the air every day. For air quality to remain high, people everywhere must take action to reduce air pollution.

The oil fires in Kuwait affected the global air system.

Darkness at Noon

An extreme example of how people have affected air quality is seen in the Kuwait oil fires. In 1991, several hundred oil wells were set afire, resulting in black soot blanketing the country of Kuwait. At one time, more than 600 oil fires were raging out of control. Scientists are undecided about the long-term impact of these fires. One hypothesis is that the burning will cause climatic changes such as increased precipitation in some parts of the world. To support this hypothesis, scientists point out that the more particles such as ash and soot from the burning oil wells there are in the air, the greater the chance for water vapor to condense onto them and cause precipitation.

How does the process of burning release substances into the air? Think about burning wood in a fireplace or campfire. Have you ever noticed the quantity of ash left behind after wood is burned? Why is this pile of ash smaller and lighter than the pile of wood that was burned? What happened to the other materials the wood contained before it burned up? Think about where they went. Would it be possible for people to burn things and not pollute the air? Do library research to answer these questions and decide how to report your findings to the class. Will you report orally? Will you create a poster or a chart detailing your discoveries?

Activity!

What Do Cars Put Into the Air?

Cars burn gasoline, releasing various substances during the process. What are the substances? Can you see them?

What You Need

meterstick, automobile, petroleum jelly, 3 paper plates, masking tape, watch with a second hand, hand lens, *Activity Log* page 26

Fasten 1 paper plate to the end of the meterstick with tape. Rub some petroleum jelly onto the paper plate, just enough to thinly cover the entire plate. Find 3 car owners who are willing to help you perform your experiment. Take 1 of them at a time to his or her car. As the adult starts the engine, hold the meterstick so that the paper plate is located a few mm behind the exhaust pipe of the car. *Safety Tip:* Be sure to stand far enough from the exhaust pipe to avoid breathing the fumes or burning yourself. Hold the plate in the exhaust fumes for 3 mins. Then remove the plate from the meterstick and label it. Describe the type of car, its age, and engine size in your *Activity Log*.

Go through the same procedure with 2 more owners and their cars. Then examine the plates with a hand lens. Describe each plate's appearance. Compare the 3 plates. Record their similarities and differences in your *Activity Log*.

In the activity you just did, you tested for only solid wastes released by burning petroleum. But burning petroleum also gives off gases such as sulfur dioxide, nitrogen oxide, and carbon monoxide. Breathing any of these substances can be damaging to your health.

Carbon monoxide, one product of burning fossil fuels, is made up of carbon and oxygen and is a deadly, invisible gas that can attach to your red corpuscles—the red blood cells that carry oxygen throughout your body. In fact, carbon monoxide attaches to red corpuscles at exactly the spots where oxygen molecules usually attach themselves, which prevents oxygen molecules from attaching. There isn't room. Your body is then deprived of the oxygen needed to keep you alive. That's why breathing large

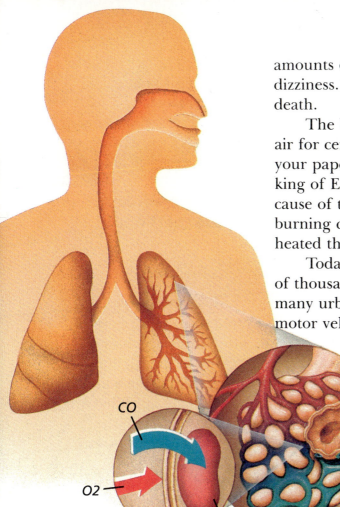

amounts of carbon monoxide can cause headaches and dizziness. Overexposure to this gas can even lead to death.

The burning of fossil fuels has contaminated the air for centuries with the same substances found on your paper plates. In the early 1300s, Edward I, then king of England, passed a law against burning coal because of the terrible smell it produced. The penalty for burning coal was death. At that time, most people heated their homes and cooked by burning wood.

Today, coal-fired power plants give off hundreds of thousands of tons of sulfur dioxide each year. In many urban areas, most air pollution comes from motor vehicles. They put more than seven million metric tons (about eight million tons) of nitrogen oxide into the air every year. Sulfur dioxide and nitrogen oxide combine in the atmosphere with other substances to form sulfuric acid and nitric acid. Eventually, these acids combine with water vapor and fall to Earth's surface as acid rain. Acid rain is very damaging. It can erode stone, concrete, metals, paint, leather, and cloth. Acid rain can also reduce crop yields and damage trees. Is all rain acidic? To test the rain in your area, do the activity on the next page.

CO

O2

Red corpuscle

Carbon monoxide can cause your body to be deprived of oxygen by attaching to the red corpuscles.

The air in England was also contaminated during the Industrial Revolution.

Activity!

How Acidic Is the Rain in Your Area?

What You Need

pH paper, beaker, distilled water, fresh rainwater,
Activity Log **page 28**

Place the beaker outside when it's raining to catch some rainwater. When a few mL of rainwater have fallen into the beaker, bring it inside. Predict which water type (rainwater or distilled water) will be more acidic. Test the pH of the distilled water by dipping a strip of pH paper into the distilled water. Record your findings in your *Activity Log*. Then, do the same with the rainwater. Which water was more acidic? Why?

Minds On! As you've discovered, the atmosphere of Earth is greatly affected by activities of people. What activities can you think of that pollute the air? In your *Activity Log* on page 27, make a list of everyday activities you do that pollute the air. What are some ways to reduce the pollution from these activities? Compare your answers with those of others. Save your list to use later. ●

Something you may not have considered as causing air pollution is the everyday use of household appliances. **Chlorofluorocarbons** (klôr ə flôr′ ə kär bənz) (CFCs)—manufactured gases containing carbon, chlorine, and fluorine—are released by various appliances. CFCs are used mostly in refrigerators, freezers, air conditioners, insulation, and water-purification devices. (Aerosol spray devices used to contain them, but CFCs are now banned from most sprays.) When these gases are released into the air, they rise into the atmosphere and destroy the ozone layer. The **ozone layer** is a layer in the atmosphere that filters out 95 to 99 percent of the sun's damaging ultraviolet rays.

Scientists have recently found holes in the ozone layer—holes they hypothesize are caused by CFCs. Because of these holes, the sun's rays may cause twice as many deaths from skin cancer over the next 50 years. Ultraviolet rays can also damage the eyes, weaken the body's immune system, and damage plant life.

Alabaster Sphinx in Memphis, Egypt

Caryatids on the Acropolis in Athens, Greece

Statues such as these have been damaged due to acid rain.

Music/Art Link

Save Our Artwork

Statue from Field Museum in Chicago, Illinois

Since acid rain can damage even stone and concrete, statues that were created by ancient sculptors are being damaged. These works of art weather naturally in wind and precipitation, but this natural process is extremely slow. Experts estimate that acid rain has caused more damage to ancient statues in the last 50 years than age and weathering have in the past 1,000 years!

Conduct some research. Find out about statues that have been damaged by airborne sulfuric or nitric acid. Focus your research on one particular statue. Find out its name, the name of the artist who created it, where it is located, how old it is, the subject it represents, and any other facts you can. Then describe how the airborne acid has altered it. Share your findings with the class.

Laws To Improve Our Air's Quality

*F*or years, people lived with air the way it was. Then some countries and even some states decided to provide standards for cleaner air by making laws. One example is the Clean Air Act, a law that requires pollutants to be reduced to safe levels in the atmosphere.

Some states require automobile emission systems that reduce both solid particles and gases that pollute and form smog, or thick clouds of pollutants. Today, a properly tuned car should emit less than one percent of carbon monoxide under normal driving conditions. Cars built since 1980 are equipped with electronic exhaust catalysts, or catalytic converters, that protect the atmosphere when maintained at manufacturers' specifications.

Automobiles are largely responsible for many air pollution problems.

In this temperature inversion over Denver, Colorado, a layer of cool air moved in under the warm air. Since the cool layer can't rise through the warm air above, the cool layer becomes trapped along with the pollutants it contains.

Since the 1970s, federal and state authorities have considered automobile air pollution to be a serious health problem. Because of auto emission standards, improvements have occurred. According to the United States Environmental Protection Agency (EPA), 1990 model cars run 96 percent cleaner than 1970 models.

Car built before 1970

Substitute car fuels are also used to prevent pollution. The best known substitute fuels are methanol and ethanol. These substances need less air to burn than gasoline does. Such fuels may soon be required by law. Other alternatives for the near future to using gasoline are electricity, natural gas, and hydrogen.

Minds On! As a group, brainstorm ideas for new inventions to stop air pollution. Design one such invention, draw a simple sketch of it in your *Activity Log* on page 29, and describe how it works to the teacher. ●

Car built after 1970

Products such as air-filtration devices, ionizers, and oxidators are all inventions designed to clean the air. Manufacturers continue to design new products to protect the air, such as emission-control devices that regulate automobile exhaust fumes.

How do the emission systems of these cars differ?

Car of the future

SCIENCE TECHNOLOGY AND Society

Focus on Technology

Pollution Emitters on Film

One way of monitoring emissions from cars is with a pollution camera. Concealed inside traffic cones, video cameras are attached to monitors that record the license plates of cars emitting 100 or more grams of carbon monoxide per 1.6 kilometers (about 3.5 ounces per mile), well over the limits set by the Clean Air Act. Citations are then mailed to violators, who must have their cars serviced to stop the high emissions.

The remote emissions monitor was designed by a University of Denver chemistry professor. It can test up to 1,200 cars per hour, day or night, in any weather. The device shoots parallel beams of infrared light through the exhaust fumes from the tailpipes of passing cars. The exhaust gases alter the beams' wavelengths. The beams are reflected to a small, polygon-shaped detection unit. It takes less than a second to determine a car's emissions. Although many states require annual emissions tests for vehicles, the tests generally used are inconvenient and perhaps not as accurate because they are performed at idling speeds, not on the highway. This new invention may soon provide faster, more accurate emissions tests.

With a small group of students, prepare a debate on this new invention. Could it be misused? Should its use be regulated or limited in any way? Should every motor vehicle be required to pass a yearly emissions test? Conduct your debate for the class.

Remote emissions monitors can be a very effective tool in controlling auto emissions.

68

Cars' emissions are monitored because of the large amount of pollutants that are given off when petroleum is burned. But using petroleum as fuel for car engines isn't the only way humans burn fossil fuels.

The sky's the limit as people around the world work toward cleaner air. From substituting cleaner fuels that power cars to video cameras that catch cars emitting too much carbon monoxide, a response is never too late to improve air quality.

Sum It Up

"Fresh" air is not as common as once thought. It is no longer taken for granted. As you discovered in the Explore Activity, there are many particles present in the air. Technology and increases in Earth's human population have led to an increase in air pollution. Now, both technology and human populations must turn to improving the quality of our air. Since Earth's atmosphere is a system of interacting masses of air, air from all around the world affects you. Clean air is a global concern, and global action is beginning to occur. Each one of us must contribute to the "clean-up effort" by respecting this vital natural resource and working to protect air quality. By doing so, we help maintain the stable and healthy environment needed for life on Earth.

Critical Thinking

1. List three or more things you can do personally to reduce air pollution.
2. In addition to increasing precipitation, how might the oil fires in Kuwait affect Earth's climate?
3. How do trees reduce air pollution?
4. List two kinds of "natural" air pollution.
5. Explain how a temperature inversion can be reversed.

Will Earth's riches be here for future generations to enjoy?

Balancing Our Natural Resources

As you studied about soil, forests, minerals, water, and air and how they affect you and are affected by your actions, did you begin to see how Earth really is like a spaceship, a self-contained vehicle traveling through space for thousands and thousands of years? Earth's natural processes continue to operate in ways that benefit both plant and animal life.

Do you remember that renewable resources are those that can be replaced within an average lifetime? The air you breathe is a renewable resource, which is continuously recycled and replaced by clean air. Non-renewable resources, those that can't be replaced within a person's lifetime, include soil, fossil fuels, and mineral deposits. Once they're used up, they're gone. Can you understand why we have reason to be concerned and to plan options for the future?

If Earth's resources are not used wisely, they could run out. That's why all of us need to plan our use of these natural resources if we're going to conserve them for future generations.

Perhaps you weren't aware of how easy it is to use energy all the time without even realizing it, but now you may have a greater awareness. You've learned that most of the electricity we use today comes from power plants using fossil fuels such as coal. And you know that Earth has a limited supply of coal.

Compost pile

The world's supply of fossil fuels is dwindling simply because of our continuing great demand. Reserves that took millions of years to form could be used up in a period of just a few hundred years! It's time for all of us to begin to think about the future stability of Earth.

Throughout this unit, you've been making a compost pile. How does a compost project illustrate a balance for the resources of Earth? How can others benefit from using compost piles? What do you predict would happen if everyone used compost piles to recycle kitchen scraps and lawn and garden refuse? The use of compost piles may play a very important part in conserving Earth's resources.

You can now discuss ideas with your friends and family and begin to formulate your adult opinion on environmental issues. What will you do when Earth's limited resources are gone? Should more time, money, and effort be spent on developing alternative energy resources?

As you look ahead, do you think Earth's landfills will ever be too full? If you answered "yes," then what can you do to put off that day? A whole new industry has been created in your lifetime because of recycling. Now plants are needed to process materials such as aluminum cans and bottles.

In this unit, you learned that people working individually and together can affect Earth's riches. What part will you play?

Your Own Part To Play

Read the following story to see how the people of one town must work together to protect the delicate balance of Earth's natural resources.

"For 50 years, the Midwest town of Maysville had looked pretty much the same—a small town, friendly people, modest, well-kept neighborhoods with backyard gardens and front porch swings.

Bordered on three sides by corn and soybean crops, Maysville's southern boundary was a section of the 100-mile long Curly River, on whose banks families loved to picnic while they fished the clear waters. But Curly River doesn't run so clear any more.

In the past, life in Maysville pretty much centered around school-sponsored events, 4-H activities, and the county fair, which brought together townspeople and those from the outlying farmland.

The children of the town had always been at the center of activities. Besides the fact that the people believed in families, there wasn't much else to do in Maysville.

Then, word began to spread among the local citizens that ActionCo, a mid-sized manufacturer of wheelchairs and other useful devices for the handicapped, had bought the old TypeCom plant and would be bringing its company to Maysville to reopen the plant!

Naturally, this was good news for those who had stayed in this sleepy little town. There had been plenty of late-night discussion among parents, neighbors, and friends about the need for work closer to home. For most of the

citizen's of Maysville, it had been a painful experience when TypeCom had announced its decision to shut down the town's 75-year-old printing plant three years earlier, giving many of them their last regular paychecks.

So, Maysville's future definitely looked brighter with the reopening of the town's new industry, ActionCo. In fact, most of the town was there the day the mayor and the 4-H princess cut the ribbon to open the town's newest facility!

Now, 14 month's later, ActionCo has definitely meant a lot of changes for Maysville, affecting more than just those who now work at jobs at the facility.

While Mayor Miller is still happy that ActionCo offers employment for 175 local citizens, he's concerned about the

change in the environment. Townspeople have slowly begun to make him aware of a change in Curly River. Could there be pollution from the new plant?

Mike Ramirez, a father of three, loves his new job. It means that at last he can buy the things his family needs. He thinks maybe a little environmental change here or there isn't too bad. He won't even discuss the potential problem.

Billy Brown, 12, who was born with spina bifida, had no idea of the range of activities available to him until ActionCo came to town, bringing wonderful new devices that support his body, so that he is even able to try sports for the first time.

Jenny Tall Pines sits next to Billy in school, and she is happy with his new-found mobility. However, she knows that some companies can cause accidental air and water pollution that can have far-ranging effects. She thinks the adults should do something about the problem before it gets worse.

The ActionCo officials have made no statements, because, frankly, they're surprised by the pollution problem. They'd made an honest effort to bring the old factory up to today's environmental standards.

Donald Maxfield is the state inspector who approved the opening of ActionCo. Had he missed something? Will he lose his job? Should he reopen the inspection report and go back for another look?

Susan Strater works as a reporter for the *Maysville Daily Gazette*. She continues to write articles for the paper urging an investigation, because she fears for the town's future.

Angela Parker believes in the innovative designs that ActionCo has brought to life. She knows that many people with handicaps benefit because of the appliances the company markets. But she's confused about the hazy, smoky skies that blow toward her neighborhood from the plant. Should she do something? She wonders whom she should ask about the problem.

There are many other living things affected by the pollution creeping into the life of Maysville—the fish in Curly River, the wildflowers on the banks of the river, the homeowners in the area surrounding the new industry, the crops struggling to grow in the acres of adjacent farmland."

Now, act out the many characters described in this story. Choose a character for yourself. It can be a person named, a person you invent, or even a plant or animal. These characters will now be involved in a town meeting. Ideas, problems, and solutions will be presented. Prepare a statement for your character to make at the meeting. Through this activity, you may begin to understand how a town can be divided over such complex environmental issues.

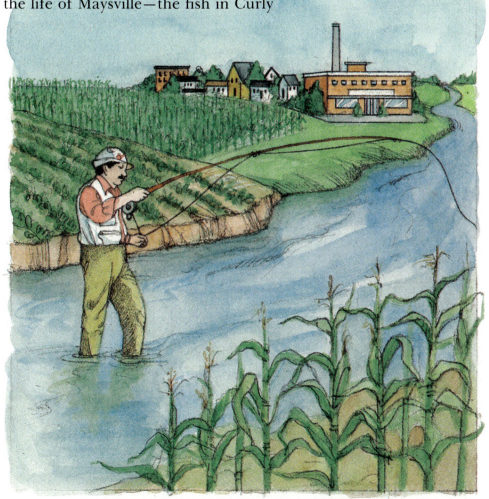

GLOSSARY

Use the pronunciation key below to help you decode, or read, the pronunciations.

Pronunciation Key

a	at, bad	d	dear, soda, bad
ā	ape, pain, day, break	f	five, defend, leaf, off, cough, elephant
ä	father, car, heart	g	game, ago, fog, egg
âr	care, pair, bear, their, where	h	hat, ahead
e	end, pet, said, heaven, friend	hw	white, whether, which
ē	equal, me, feet, team, piece, key	j	joke, enjoy, gem, page, edge
i	it, big, English, hymn	k	kite, bakery, seek, tack, cat
ī	ice, fine, lie, my	l	lid, sailor, feel, ball, allow
îr	ear, deer, here, pierce	m	man, family, dream
o	odd, hot, watch	n	not, final, pan, knife
ō	old, oat, toe, low	ng	long, singer, pink
ô	coffee, all, taught, law, fought	p	pail, repair, soap, happy
ôr	order, fork, horse, story, pour	r	ride, parent, wear, more, marry
oi	oil, toy	s	sit, aside, pets, cent, pass
ou	out, now	sh	shoe, washer, fish mission, nation
u	up, mud, love, double	t	tag, pretend, fat, button, dressed
ū	use, mule, cue, feud, few	th	thin, panther, both
ü	rule, true, food	th	this, mother, smooth
u̇	put, wood, should	v	very, favor, wave
ûr	burn, hurry, term, bird, word, courage	w	wet, weather, reward
ə	about, taken, pencil, lemon, circus	y	yes, onion
b	bat, above, job	z	zoo, lazy, jazz, rose, dogs, houses
ch	chin, such, match	zh	vision, treasure, seizure

aerate (âr′ āt′):   to supply with air.

biodegrade (bī′ ō di grād′):   to break down into simpler components by the action of microorganisms or other living things.

carbon dioxide (kär′ bən dī ok′ sīd):   a colorless gas made up of carbon and oxygen atoms.

chemical weathering (kem′ i kəl weth′ ər ing):   a process that breaks down the chemical composition of minerals and rocks.

chlorofluorocarbon (CFCs) (klôr′ ə flür′ ə kär′ bən):   a chemical that contains chlorine, fluorine, and carbon.

deforestation (dē′ fôr is tā′ shən):   the process of completely clearing forest lands.

forest: a dense growth of trees and underbrush that covers a large area of land.

fossil fuel (fos′ əl fū′ əl):   a fuel such as coal, petroleum, and natural gas formed from the decay of organisms that lived millions of years ago.

groundwater: water beneath Earth's surface that may supply wells and springs.

humus (hū′ məs):   material formed from decayed organic matter; found in topsoil.

hydrocarbon (hī′ drə kär bən):   a compound that is composed of carbon and hydrogen.

leaching (lēch ing):   the process by which some soil components are dissolved and carried downward by water.

metallic mineral (mə tal′ ik min′ ər əl): a mineral that has a shiny metal - like appearance.

mineral (min′ ər əl):   a naturally occurring, inorganic, crystalline solid with a definite chemical composition.

natural gas: a clean - burning fossil fuel formed from decayed marine organisms.

nonmetallic mineral: a mineral that has a dull appearance.

oil reservoir (oil rez′ ər vwär′):   an underground supply of petroleum that can be drilled for oil.

ozone layer (ō′ zōn lā′ ər):   a region of the atmosphere consisting of O_3, a type of oxygen molecule that absorbs most of the ultraviolet radiation entering the atmosphere.

percolate (pûr′ kə lāt′):   to drain or seep through a permeable substance.

permeability (pûr′ mē ə bil′ i tē):   a condition of some rocks in which connecting pore spaces exist within the rock, thus allowing fluids to move through the rock.

physical weathering (fiz′ i kəl we<u>th</u>′ ər ing):   a process in which rocks and minerals are broken apart mechanically.

rock: Earth material made of one or more minerals.

runoff (run′ ôf′):   the precipitation that runs over Earth's surface instead of sinking in; precipitation that eventually reaches streams and rivers.

soil: a mixture of weathered rock and decayed organic material.

soil erosion (soil i rō′ zhən):   a process that removes soil from an area.

soil horizons (soil hə rī′ zənz):   layers in the soil that differ from one another in chemical, physical, and biological composition.

soil profile (soil prō′ fīl):   a vertical section of all soil horizons that make the soil.

strip mining: a method of obtaining minerals, ores, or fossil fuel from near Earth's surface by cutting trenches into the land.

transpiration (tran′ spə rā′ shən):   the process of losing water vapor to the air from a living organism through a membrane or pores.

water table: the upper edge of material underground completely saturated with groundwater.

zone of saturation (sach′ ə rā′ shən):   an underground area that lies above an impermeable layer and contains water within its pores; the area directly below the water table.

INDEX

CREDITS